ISBN 978-1-331-71897-0
PIBN 10225707

For support please visit www.forgottenbooks.com

1 MONTH OF
FREE
READING

at
www.ForgottenBooks.com

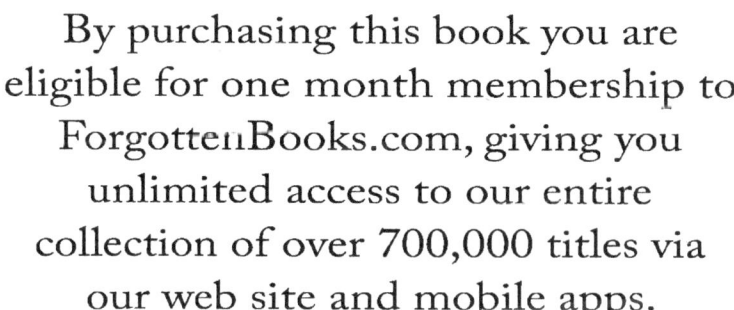

By purchasing this book you are eligible for one month membership to ForgottenBooks.com, giving you unlimited access to our entire collection of over 700,000 titles via our web site and mobile apps.

To claim your free month visit:
www.forgottenbooks.com/free225707

The

𝔞𝔰𝔱 𝔄𝔤 𝔬𝔣 𝔱𝔥 𝔆𝔥𝔦 𝔯 𝔥

By J O H N W Y C L Y F F E.

Now first Printed

𝔉 𝔬𝔪 𝔞 𝔐𝔬 𝔲𝔰𝔠 𝔭𝔱

In the

UNIVERSITY LIBRARY, DUBLIN.

EDITED WITH NOTES,

By

JAMES HENTHORN TODD, D D.,

Fellow of Trinity College, and Treasurer of St. Patrick's Cathedral.

𝔇𝔲𝔟𝔩𝔦𝔫 :

AT THE UNIVERSITY PRESS.

M.DCCC.XL.

¶ The Preface.

———◆———

 Well known popular Writer on the History of the Christian Church has given it as his Opinion, that whoever will carefully examine the original Records, will soon be convinced that the Merits of *Wyclyffe*, as a Reformer, have been considerably exaggerated. How far this is true or not, the Writer of these Pages will not attempt to determine ; but certain it is,

Milner,
Hist. of the
Church, vol.
iv. p. 121.
Lond. 1819.

that to " examine the original Records," ·
with a View to discover the real Doctrines
and Opinions of *Wyclyffe*, is much more
easily said than done; and the Reader
who seeks for Satisfaction from the Biographers of the Reformer, or from the Histo-
rians of the Period, will soon be convinced
that the original Records, and above all,
the still remaining Writings of *Wyclyffe*
and his Followers, have never been examined with the Care and Attention necessary for the Purpose of forming a just
Estimate of his Opinions, and of the Merit
of his Efforts at a Reformation of the
Church.

The List of *Wyclyffe's* Writings pub-

lished by Bishop *Bale,* in his Work, *Scrip-* Cent. vi. p.
450.
torum Majoris Brytanniæ Catalogus, has
been necessarily made the Basis of all that
subsequent Writers have collected. It The Hist. of
the Life of
has been reprinted, with many useful ad- John *Wiclif,*
D.D. By
ditions, by the learned and indefatigable John *Lewis,*
M.A. Oxf.
John Lewis, of whose Labours every 1820.
Student must speak with Gratitude. Mr. Memoirs of
Wiclif, By
Baber also has done much towards assisting the Rev.
H. H. Ba-
future Inquirers, by the very valuable *ber,* M.A.
4to. Lond.
List of the Reformer's Writings that he 1810.
has compiled. Here, however, we must
stop ; Mr. *Vaughan's* Compilation has The Life
of *John de*
not added much to our Knowledge of *Wycliffe,*
D.D. By
the Subject, nor can it be commended *Robert*
Vaughan.
either for Accuracy or Learning ; and Lond. 1831.

The Life of
Wiclif. By
Chas. W. Le
Bas, M.A.
Lond. 1832.

Mr. *Le Bas* does not profess to do more than follow his Predecessors. His humbler Task, however, has been executed with great Elegance and Judgment.

The Truth, therefore, is, that until the Works of *Wyclyffe*, real and supposititious, be collected and published, it is vain to talk of determining his Opinions, or fixing his real Merits as a Reformer; and it is with the Hope of directing Attention to this Subject that the following Tract

Appendix
ad Histor.
Litterar. Cl.
V. *Gul.*
Cave. vol. ii.
p. 63. Fol.
Oxon. 1743.

is now printed. The learned *Henry Wharton* was willing to believe that all the Writings of *Wyclyffe* might in his Time have been recovered: "*omnia* Wiclefi scripta," he says, " *in Anglia adhuc deli-*

tescere, et ex Bibliothecis nostris qua pub-licis qua privatis in lucem erui posse, lubenter crederem." Perhaps we have still all the MSS. that existed in *Wharton's* Time, and it may be still within our Power to rescue them from the Oblivion in which they have so long been suffered to remain. But the Chances of their De-struction are every Day becoming greater, and Delay in such an Enterprize is highly dangerous. It is true that many of these Documents will be found dry, and to the popular Reader uninteresting; buried in the barbarous Latinity of the Schools, or concealed under the perhaps still more ob-solete English of the fourteenth Century.

But they who would engage in such a Labour as the Publication of the Works of *Wyclyffe*, must be above the narrow Influences of modern Utilitarianism. They must keep in View a higher Field of Learning than comes within the Sphere of Mercantile Speculators in Literature, or Useful Knowledge Societies. They must feel that the Value of these Documents as Compositions, is but a secondary Object in their Publication; the great End must be the Discovery of Truth, and the Preservation of the Remains of an illustrious Character in our History. What nobler, what more imperishable Monument could the Gratitude of England raise to her first

Reformer, than a complete and uniform Edition of his extant Writings ?

The Editor is fully sensible that the Tract which is now for the first Time given to the public, is very far from being a favorable Specimen of the Works of *Wyclyffe.* But it commended itself for Publication on many Grounds : First, its Shortness. Secondly, its early Date ; for it bears internal Evidence of having been composed in the Year 1356, and must, therefore, (if really by *Wyclyffe,*) have been the earliest See *Page* xxxi. of his Writings. Another Motive for publishing this Production is furnished by the Consideration, that, if it be genuine, it reveals to us a Fact not dwelt upon, so far

as the Editor knows, by any of the Reformer's Biographers; namely, the Connexion which existed between the earlier
Doctrines of *Wyclyffe*, and the prophetical Speculations of the *Beguins*, circulated
under the *N*ame of the famous Abbot
Joachim.

It remains, however, to be proved, that
the Tract now printed is really *Wyclyffe's*;
and this, the Editor admits, seemed to
him an additional Reason for selecting it
for Publication; inasmuch as it served at
once to raise the Question, How far we
have certain Grounds for attributing to
Wyclyffe the Writings that exist under
his *N*ame; nor is it perhaps too much

to say, that this is a Subject which the learned World has never been in a Condition to consider fully. Yet there is no preliminary Question more deserving of Attention, if we would form a just Estimate of our Reformer's Merits; for it must be evident to every reflecting Reader, that if we are in any Degree uncertain of the Genuineness of such Writings as are quoted under the Name of *Wyclyffe*, the Conclusions drawn from them, as to the Nature and Character of his Doctrines, must be in the same Degree uncertain, and destitute of Authority.

In the present Case, the Grounds upon which the following Treatise has been assigned to *Wyclyffe*, are no more than these :—First, that it is found in a MS. Volume of the fourteenth Century, which contains several other Tracts, that are believed to be *Wyclyffe's*. Secondly, that it has been ascribed to *Wyclyffe*, by Bishop *Bale*, Mr. *Lewis*, and, after them, by his more modern Biographers.

These Remarks are not made with a Design to cast any Doubt on the Genuineness of the following Treatise. It is very probably by *Wyclyffe*, although we have no better Reason than the Authority of *Bale* for thinking so. But if any Reader should entertain a Doubt on this Subject, deeming the Tract unworthy of our Reformer, (as many will doubtless feel it to be very different from what they would have expected from the Pen of *Wyclyffe*,) the Editor must confess himself unable to satisfy such Scruples ; nor is he aware of any Argument by which the Authority of *Bale* and *Lewis* can be supported. The Conclusion, however, to which he desires to bring the Reader, and for the Sake of which he has hazarded these Remarks, is simply this, that until the various Treatises attributed to *Wyclyffe* are collected, and rendered accessible to the Learned, it is vain to think of deciding the Question how far any given Tract is worthy or unworthy of his Pen.

One other Particular, concerning the following Work, remains to be considered.

Vaughan's Life of Wycliffe. Vol. i. p. 255. Note. 2nd Edit. Mr. *Vaughan* tells us that " this is one of the Reformer's Pieces that is to be found only in the Library of Trinity College, Dublin ·" and this may, for aught we know, be true, although perhaps it only means that no other Copy of the Tract was elsewhere found by Mr. *Vaughan.* Certain, however, it is, that Bishop *Bale* has entered the Treatise in two different Places of his Catalogue, and under two different Titles ; from which we may infer, that in his Time, or in the Times of those from whom he copied, the Tract was found in two different Collec-

tions. In one place he enters it thus :— *Balæus*, De
Script.
(See *No.* 84 of *Lewis's* Catalogue.) Brytanniæ.
Cent. vi. p.
453.
" *De simonia sacerdotum,* lib. 1. *Heu magni*
Lewis, Life
sacerdotes in tenebris." of *Wiclif*,
p. 195.

In another place he gives it the Title *Bale*, U. S.
p. 454.
under which it is now published, and de- *Lewis*, p.
205. No.
scribes it thus :— 148.

" *De ultimâ ætate Ecclesiæ,* lib. 1. *Sacerdotes,*
proh dolor! versantes in vitiis."

It is by no means improbable, therefore,
that a second Copy of the Tract may still
exist, under some Disguise, in our public
or private Libraries.

The Volume from which the Treatise
is now printed, is preserved among the

MSS. of Archbishop *Ussher*, in the Library of the University of *Dublin*. It appears to have been once the Property of Sir *Robert Cotton*, whose Autograph is found on the lower Margin of the first See *Nichols'* Autographs, Plate 44. No. 5. Page, in his usual Form of Signature:

      " *Robert Cotton Bruceus.*"

On the upper Margin of the same Page, in a Hand of the early Part of the sixteenth Century, now nearly obliterated, may be traced the Words,

  " *Wiclefe roas a thousand thre hūderyd thre schorr and uiij.*"

Over which Sir *Robert Cotton* has written,

"*Anno* 1368. *Wicklif workes to the Duk of Lancaster.*"

Nothing appears in the Volume to indicate the exact Year in which it was transcribed, but the Hand-writing would lead us to assign it to the latter End of the fourteenth or Beginning of the fifteenth Century. It is imperfect in some places, but contains a very valuable Col lection of the Tracts of *Wyclyffe,* for a complete List of which the Reader is referred to some Papers that were published in the Year 1835, in the *British Maga-* zine ; where he will also find an Account of the Treatise, now for the first time printed, " On the last Age of the

British Magazine, *vol.* vii. p. 532, and p. 690. *Vol.* viii. p. 267, and p. 402.

Chirche," with an Exposure of certain Mistakes that have been committed respecting it. Several of the Remarks contained in those Papers have been transferred to the *N*otes, which will be found at the End of the present Volume.

¶ The last Age of the Chirche By John Wyclyffe, S. Th P.

M.ccc.luj.

The Last Age

of the

Chirche.

Las forsorwe grete pres=
tis sittinge in derkenessis &
in schadewe of deep/ noʒt
hauynge him pat openly
criep/ al pis I wille ʒeue ʒif
pou auaunce me. Pei make reseruaciouns/
pe whiche ben clepid dymes/ ffirst fruytis/
oper penciouns/ aftir pe oppynioun of
hem pat trete pis matir.   ffor no more

schulde ſatte beneficis be reſerued p̄ne
smale/ ȝif no pryuy cauſe of symonye
were tretide/ þe whiche I ſeie noȝt at

Joachim.

þis tyme. But Joachur/ in his book of
þe ſeedis of profetis ⁊ of þe ſeyingis of
popes ⁊ of þe chargis of profetis/ tretynge
þis matir/ ⁊ spekynge of þe rente of dymes/

Psal. 90.

ſeiþ þus/ foure tribulaciouns Daniþ þe
profete haþ biſore ſeid/ þe ſeuynty ⁊ nyue
chapitre/ to entre into þe Chirche of God/

Bernard.

⁊ Bernard acordiþ þere wiþ/ vpon can=
tica/ þe pre ⁊ pritty sermon/ þat ben/ a
nyȝtly drede/ an arwe fleynge in day/
chaffare walkynge in derkenessis/ ⁊ myd=
dais deuylrie/ þat is to ſeye/ antecrist.
Nyȝtly drede was whanne alle þat ſlowen
ſeyntis demyd hem ſilf do ſerupſe to

God/ ꝗ þis was þe firste tribulacionn þat
ontrede þe Chirche of God. Þₑ arwe fleynge
in day was descept of heretikis/ ꝗ þat
was þe secunde tribulacioun þat entred þe
Chirche of Crist. Þat is put of bi wisdom
of seyntis/ as þe firste was cast out bi
stedfastenesse of martiris. Chaffare walk=
ynge in derkenessis is þe pryui heresie of
symonyans/ bi resoun of whiche þe pridde
tribulacionn schal entre into Cristis
Chirche/ þe whiche tribulacioun or an=
gusch schal entre þe Chirche of Crist in
þe tyme of þe hundrid ȝeer of .x. lettre/ whos
ende we ben/ as I wele prene/ ꝗ þis mys=
cheif schal be so heuy þat wel schal be
to þat man of holy Chirche þat p̄ne schal
noȝt be on lyue. And þat I preue þus

D

Joachim· bi Joachrin in his book of þe deedis of profetis. Men of ebren tunge haneþ xxii lettris/ and byngynge fro þe first of ebrew lettris/ & zeuynge to euery lettre an hundrid zeer/ þe oolde Testament was endid whāne þe noumbre zeuen to þe lettris was fulfillid. So fro þe bygynnynge of ebrew lettris in to Crist/ in þe whiche þe oolde Testament was endid/ weren two and twenty hundriddis of zeeris. Þis also [he] schewiþ openly bi discripcioun of tyme/ of

Eusebi. Bede. Haymound. Eusebi/ Bede/ & Haymound/ most preued of acounteris/ or talkeris. So Cristen men hauen xxi lettris/ & bygynnynge fro þe first of Latyn lettris/ & zeuynge to eche .c./ þe newe Testament was endid whanne þe noumbre of þes as-

singned lettris was fulfillid. And þis is as
soþ as in þe bigynnynge God made
heuene ⁊ erþe/ for þe oolde Testament is
figur of þe newe.   But aftir Joachim ⁊ _{Joachim.}
Bede/ fro þe bygynnynge of Latyn lettris _{Bede.}
to þe comynge of Crist weren senene hun=
drid ȝeere/ so þat Crist cam in þe hondrid
of .h'. lettre/ Crist steye to heuene/ and
aftir þat/ undir .k'. lettre/ Crist delyuered
his Chirche fro nyȝtly drede/ þe whiche was
þe firste drede þat Goddis Chirche was inne.
Aftir þat/ vndir .m. lettir/ Crist delyuered
his Chirche fro þe arwe fleynge in day/
þat was þe secunde tribulacioun of þe
Chirche/ ⁊ þat was demynge by Joachim _{Joachim.}
⁊ oþere þat vndir .m. lettre schewede þe
multitude of heretikis contraryinge þe

birpe of Crist his pascioun ꝸ his assen=
cioun/ in þat þat .m. lettre most figured
Crist.   Euery lettre in þe abece may be
sonned wiþ opyn monþ sane .m. lettre one/
þe whiche may noȝt be sonned but wiþ
clos mouþ. So Crist myȝte noȝt come out
of þe maydenes wombe/ but sche hadde be
clos.   And þes ben uerse of .m. lettre/

College claustris exire solent patefactis/
Una sed ex istis nō egreditur nisi clausis.

Aftir þat/ budir .x. lettre/ was þe
pridde tribulacioun in Goddis Chirche/
þe whiche .x. lettre is last of Latyn lettris/
ꝸ þe pridde tribulacioun schal be schewid
in þe hondrid ȝeere of .x. lettre.   I preue
it bi two resouns/ þe firste is þis. Petir

þe Apostle þe whiche was in þe tyme
of .I. lettre/ myȝte not bttirly distrie
Symoun Magus/ but bi helpe of Poul/ Act. 8.
þe whiche was þe pritteneþ Apostil. So/
ȝif .x. lettre be þe pritteneþe fro .I. lettre/
in þe tyme of .x. lettre Crist schal clanse
his Chirche fro marchaundise walkynge
in derkenessis. Þe secuude resoun is suche.
Ȝit cam noȝt þat tribulacioun þat schal be
in Goddis Chirche bi canse of chaffare
walkynge in derkenesses/ ⁊ þat þat is pro=
phesied schal come. Sippe þanne þat we
ben in .x. lettre/ as it is schewid/ þis tri=
bulacioun schal come in .x. lettre oþere
aftir/ but aftir .x. lettre/ þat is þe last of
Latyn lettris/ schal be no tribulacioun
in Goddis Chirche bote þe fourþe ⁊ þe

Antecrist.

laste/ þe whiche schal be bi þe deuel of mydday/ þat is Antecrist/ þe whiche tribulacioun bi no Latyn lettre may be certefied/ as þes þre bifore. Ffor his comynge oonly to God is knowen/ & knowleche of him to God oonly reserued. Wherfore it folwiþ þat bndir .x. lettre schal be schewid þilke tribulacioun þat schal be in Goddis Chirche/ by resoun of chaffare walkynge in derkenessis.

Bede.
Joachim.

Þat we ben bndir þe hundrid ȝeere of .x. lettre/ I schewe schortly by Bede bpon þe profetis of Sibille/ and by Ioachim in þe book of þe seedis of profetis/ & oþere writeris of stories. Ffro þe bygynnynge of Latyn lettris to Crist Ihū/ were senene hundrid ȝeer/ and fro Crist til now/

prittene hundriþ ʒeer and sixe ⁊ fyfty/ so
þat þere ben to come of our abece but foure
⁊ fourty ʒeer/ ⁊ bi þis of þe hundriþ ʒeere
of .x. bey passiþ sixe ⁊ fifty ʒeere. Þe
synnes bi cause of whiche suche persecu=
cioun schal be in Goddis Chirche our
tyme ben þes/ for Goddis Chirche is
foundiþ in kynrade of prelatis. Þis same
rekened Ioachim in þe bookis bifore. Also
for goodis of holy Chirche þat prelatis
wiþ holdey to hem/ as pensiouns/ firste
frutis/ fermes/ prouendris/ þe whiche may
wel be clepiþ collibiste/ þes synnes and
oþere suche ben marchaundise walkynge
in derkenessis. Þe manere of tribulacioun
schal be such as Ioachim seiþ in þe book
of þe charge of profetis. Men of holy

Carnotensis, in Polycratic⁰.

Chirche schal be seyd in a manere of ca=
reyne/ þei schal be cast out as dogge in
myddis placis.   Her wiþ acordiþ Carno=
sencis/ in a book þat he clepiþ pollicrati=
con/ þe seuenþe book/ þe tenþe chapitre/ ¶
he aleyeþ Gregor seiynge þus/ pestilencis/
smyttingis to gidere of folkis/ ¶ hurtlynge
to gidere of rewmes/ ¶ oþir harmes schal
come to þe erþe/ for þat worschipis of
holy Chirche þey ȝeue to bnworþi men.

In lib. 8⁰
And in þe eiȝteþe book/ defaute of prestis
among Goddis folk bryngiþ in tirnauntis.
Þat þis tribulacioun is nyȝe/ and whanne
it schal come/ bi hem þat tretiþ þis matir
is/ whanne men schulle wante teeþ/ and
comynly alle children/ boren siþþen þe
first pestylence/ ben such þat wanten eiȝte

grete teey. Herwiþ acordiþ Merlyn Am= Merlyn Ambrose.
brose/ þat such angusche is nyʒe/ for as
by hem/ in þe tyme of þe myscheif of þe
kok/ þat we clepe fraunce/ þat schal be
distroyed by þe sixte of irlond/ þe witt is
our kyng wiþ his children. Sibille acor= Sibille.
diþ herto/ þat suche tribulacioun is nyʒe/
in þes berse :

Gallus succuutus aquile victricia signa/
Mundus adorabit/ est vrbs vix presule
  digna/
Papa cito moritur/ Sesar regnabit vbique/
Sub quo tune vana cessabit gloria cleri.

Þei þat treten þes berse of Sibille/ alle þat
I hane seen/ acorden in þis/ þat seculer
power of þe Hooly Goost elispirid/ & þat

dey/ beniaunce of swerd/ myscheifs vn-
knowe bifore/ bi whiche men þes daies
schule be ponyschid/ schulen falle for synne
of prestis. Men schal falle on hem/ ⁊
caste hem out of her fatte beneficis/ and þei
schule seye/ he cam in to his benefice by
his kynrede/ þes bi couenant maad bi-
fore/ he for his seruyse/ ⁊ þes for mo-
neye/ cam into Goddis Chirche. Þanne
schal eche suche prest erye/ Alas/ Alas/
þat no good spiryt dwellid wiþ me at my
comynge into Goddis Chirche. Þe
wordis of Josue 2. cº. þe pridde. I seide
þat Crist entrede into hooly þingis/ þat
is holy Chirche/ by holy lyuynge ⁊ holy
techinge/ preynge þe Fadir for vs. Þe
Mayster of Scholys rehersiþ/ þe pridde

Mayster of
Scholys.

book of Kyngis/ þe b. cᵒ./ aftir þe talis
of iewis of Salamon/ þere was a stork
hadde a berd/ ⁊ his berd was sperid vndir
a bessel of glas/ and whanne þis stork sau
his brid/ ⁊ þat he myȝte noȝt rome to
hym/ he brouȝt a litil reed worme out of
wildirnesse/ ⁊ wiþ his blood he anoyntide
þe glas. Þe glass to barst/ ⁊ þe brid
fleye his wey. So oure Lord þe Fadir
of heuene hadde mankynde in helle/ þat
was glasyne/ þat is to seye britil as glas.
To breke it he brouȝt suche a litil reed
worme/ þat was our Lord Jhū Crist/
as Dauiþ seiþ/ þe on ⁊ twenty Salme. 2i. Psal. 21.
Ego sum vermis/ ⁊ non homo/ I am a
worme ⁊ no man/ ⁊ wiþ his blood he
delyuered mannes kynde. Zacarie writiþ/ Zach. 9.

þe nynþe chapitre/ þou forsoþe wiþ blood
of witnesse/ or þi testament/ hast ledde
out hem þat were bounde in þe pyt. So
whanne we weren synful/ & children of
wraþþe/ Goddis sone cam out of heuene/
& preyyng his fadir for his enemyes/ &
he deyed for vs þanne/ myche raþere now
we ben maad riȝtful bi his blood schule be
saned.   Poul writiþ to þe romayns.
b. cᵒ. He schal preye for vs. Thūs
weute into heuene to apere to þe semlant
of God for vs.   Poul to þe hebrees.   Þe
whiche semlant he grannte vs
to see/ þat lyueþ & regneþ
wiþout eende/
Amen.

Rom. v.

Heb. 9.

NOTES.

Notes.

Ow far the foregoing Tract has suffered from the Carelessness or Ignorance of the Transcriber, it will not be possible to determine, until another Copy shall be discovered. It is the Object of the following Notes to correct some of the more obvious Mistakes, as well as to trace the Historical Origin of the Tract, and to explain its References and Allusions. The Editor has not thought it necessary to preserve in every Instance the Contractions of the original Manuscript; but he has carefully retained the Spelling, even in some Cases where an Error of the Transcriber is evident. The Anglo-Saxon Letters, ƿ and ȝ, are used throughout the MS., and are preserved, as being characteristic of the Orthography of the Period.

PAGE xxiii. line 3.

𝕹𝖔𝖟𝖙 𝖍𝖆𝖚𝖞𝖓𝖌𝖊 𝖍𝖎𝖒 𝖕𝖆𝖙 𝖔𝖕𝖊𝖓𝖑𝖞 𝖈𝖗𝖎𝖊𝖕.

There seems some Error or Omission of the Transcriber here; but the Allusion is probably to St. Matt. iv. 9. A learned Friend has ingeniously suggested to the Editor, that "nought-having" may mean disregarding, *pro nihilo habentes*, not fearing, abhorring, or thinking any Harm of him that openly crieth, "all these Things will I give thee, if thou wilt fall down and worship me;" i. e. not fearing the Demon of Simony. "Avaunce" is perhaps substituted for *adoraveris*, in order to render the Passage more applicable to Clerical Simony, or Purchase of Preferment.

Ibid. line 6.

𝔙ei make reseruaciouns.

The Exactions of the Court of *Rome* had been made the Subject of Legislation in *England*, from the 35 of *Edw.* I., in which Year (A.D. 1306-7) Petitions were presented to the King from the Nobility and Commonalty of the Realm against the intolerable Exactions of the Pope; (*Super variis novis et intollerabilibus gravaminibus, oppressionibus, injuriis, et extorsionibus .... auctoritate et mandato Domini Papæ;*) and these Petitions were the Occasion of a Statute, passed at a Parliament held at *Carlisle* in that Year, whereby the Papal Taxation of Abbeys and Religious

Ryley, Placita Parliam. p. 379.

Statutes of the Realm, Vol. i. Lond. 1810, p. 150.

E

Houses was restrained, and in certain Cases
prohibited. In the Year 1350-1, however,
(25 *Edw.* III.) only Six Years before the Date

Ibid. p.
316.
Gibson's
Codex, p.
65. *2nd*
Edit.

of the Tract before us, the Statute *against*
Papal Provisions of Benefices was passed,
in which the Pope's Power of presenting to
Benefices in *England*, in Violation of the Rights
of the natural Patrons, was restrained, and the
Provisors attached. The Word *Reservation*
seems to be used in the Text to denote the
Provisions prohibited by these Acts of Parliament;—it is thus defined by *Du Cange:*

Glossarium,
in voc.

" *Rescriptum seu mandatum summi Ponti-*
ficis, quo certorum beneficiorum, cum vaca-
verint, collationem sibi reservat faciendam
cui voluerit, aliis legitimis collatoribus ex-
clusis." This is exactly what the Statutes
referred to term *Provision.* The Word *Reser-*

Coke:
Part. i.
lib. ii. c.
12, sect.
215.

vation, however, is used by our modern Law-
Authorities in a more general Sense, to denote

a Rent or Profit reserved by the Owner of an Estate or Tenement for his own Use: and in this Sense the First Fruits or Annates, Tenths, and Pensions, claimed by the Court of *Rome*, are rightly termed *Reservations*, and in their Origin are clearly Simoniacal: such Pensions, First Fruits, and Tenths being in fact the Price paid to the Court of *Rome* for Collation, as appears from the Statute 13 *Ric.* II. *Stat.* 2, c. 2, (A.D. 1389-90,) where after reciting the Statutes 25 *Edw.* III. and 35 *Edw.* I. the Act goes on to complain: *Et ja monstre soit a n̄r. sr. le Roi &c.* " And now it is shewed to our Lord the King, in this present Parliament holden at *Westminster*, at the Utas of the Purification of our Lady, ... by the grievous Complaints of all the Commons of his Realm, that the Grievances and Mischiefs aforesaid do daily abound, to the great Damage and Destruction of all this

Statutes of the Realm, vol. ii. p. 70, 71. *Lond.* 1816.

E 2

Realm, more than ever were before, viz. that now of late our Holy Father the Pope, by Procurement of Clerks and otherwise, hath reserved, and doth daily reserve to his Collation, generally and especially, as well Archbishopricks, Bishopricks, Abbeys, and Priories, as all other Dignities, and other Benefices of *England*, which be of the Advowry of People of Holy Church, and doth give the same as well to Aliens as to Denizens, and taketh of all such Benefices, the First Fruits, and many other Profits, and a great Part of the Treasure of the said Realm is carried away and dispended out of the said Realm by the Purchasers of such Graces; and also by such privy Reservations many Clerks advanced in this Realm by their true Patrons, which have peaceably holden their Advancements by long Time, be suddenly put out: Whereupon, the said Commons have prayed our said Lord the

King, &c." And again, in Statute 6 *Hen.* IV.
(A.D. 1404) cap. 1. *Sur la grevouse com-* Ibid. p. 43.
pleint, &c. " For the grievous Complaints
made to our Sovereign Lord the King by his
Commons of this Parliament, holden at *Co-*
ventry, the vj. Day of October, the vj. Year of
his Reign, of the horrible Mischiefs and dam-
nable Custom which is introduct of new in the
Court of *Rome,* that no Parson, Abbot, nor
other, should have Provision of any Archbishoprick or Bishoprick, which shall be void,
till he hath compounded with the Pope's
Chamber, to pay great and excessive Sums of
Money, as well for the First Fruits of the
same Archbishoprick or Bishoprick, as for
other less Services in the same Court, and
that the same Sums, or the greater part there-
of, be paid beforehand, &c."

Thus it appears that the Exactions of the
Papal Court were attracting great Attention

in *England*, at the Period when this Tract was written. The Parliament, viewing the Matter as Politicians, denounced the Papal Claims on the Grounds that large Sums of Money were annually sent out of *England*, and Aliens advanced to spiritual Livings in the Church; *Wyclyffe* taking up the Question as a Theologian, censures these Exactions as Simoniacal, and refers to them as symptomatic of the Approach of *Antichrist*.

See *Gibson*, Codex, Tit. xxxv. p. 824. *Godolphin*, Repertorium, c. xxx. *Ayliffe*, Parergon, p. 63.

The *Dismes* mentioned in the Text are the *Decimæ Decimarum*, or Tenths of all Livings, which, with the First Fruits, were originally claimed by the Pope, although subsequently annexed to the Crown; and which now form the Foundation of the Fund called *Queen Anne's Bounty*.

The *Pensions* exacted by the Court of *Rome* were still more directly Simoniacal: they are thus alluded to in the Preamble of

an Act passed in the Reign of King *Henry* Stat. 25,
VIII., where the Commons, addressing the *Hen.* VIII.
c. 21. *Gib-*
King, say: " That where your Subjects of *son's* Codex,
this your Realm, and of other Countries and p. 87.
Dominions being under your Obeysance, by
many Years past have been, and yet be greatly
decayed and impoverished by such intolerable
Exactions of great Sums of Money as have
been claimed and taken, and yet continually
be claimed to be taken out of this your Realm,
and other your said Countries and Dominions,
by the Bishop of *Rome,* called the Pope, and
the See of *Rome,* as well in Pensions, Censes,
Peter-pence, Procurations, Fruits, Suits for
Provisions, and Expeditions of Bulls for Archbishopricks and Bishopricks, &c. . . . .

It may, therefore, please your most
noble Majesty, for the Honor of Almighty
God, &c. . . . . . . That no Person or Persons
of this your Realm, or of any other your Do-

minions, shall from henceforth pay any Pensions, Censes, Portions, Peter-pence, or any other Impositions to the Use of the said Bishop, or of the See of *Rome.*"

PAGE xxiv. line 2.

smale.

This Word in the MS. is written apparently "samle," which must be an Error. The Editor has ventured to adopt a conjectural Emendation, and print it " smale," i. e. *small.* This, at least, will make Sense; for, the Author's Argument is, that if there were nothing of a Simoniacal Nature in the Reservation of Benefices, the small Benefices would be as often made the Subjects of the Papal Provisions and Reservations, as the " fatte" or more valuable Livings; but the contrary being the Case, it follows that the Income of the Benefice is the real Object, and, therefore, that all these Exactions of the Court of *Rome* are Si- moniacal in their Origin.

Ibid. line 4.

𝔍oacḥur.

An evident mistake of the Scribe for *Joa- chim.* In another Place, by a different Er- ror, we find the Abbot called *Joachrin.* See p. xxvi.

Ibid.

𝔍n ḥis book of þe seeḋis of profetis, &c.

Whether one Book or more be here referred to seems doubtful. The Editor is disposed to think that three different Works are intended; —the first, *Of the Seedis of Profetis;* the second, *Of the Seyingis of Popes ;* and the third, *Of the Chargis of Profetis.* In another Place (p. xxvi) we find *Joachim* quoted " in his Book *of the Deedis of Profetis ;*" and (p. xxix) " *Joachim* in the Book *of the Seedis of Prophetis.*" Again (p. xxx) " the *Bookis*" of *Joachim* are spoken of in the plural Number, and " the Book *Of the Charge of Prophetis*" is quoted, as distinct from the rest.

It is probable that the Book *of the Seedis of Profetis,* and the Book *of the Deedis of Profetis,* may be the same; the Word *Deedis* or *Seedis* being one or other of them a Mistake of the Transcriber. If the Word *Seedis* be correct, the Title of the Work was probably *De seminibus prophetarum ;* unless we take *Seedis,* as derived from the Verb *to say,* for *dicta ;* for which there seems no Authority, especially as we find *Seyingis* used to express *dicta*, in the very Passage before us. From the other Reading, the Title of the Book would be *De gestis prophetarum*. The Book *Of the Seyingis of Popes* may, perhaps, be meant for the *Liber de Flore* of the Abbot Joachim, which the Author of his Life tells us was also called *De summis pontificibus.* _{Vit. *Joach.* c. v. *Acta Sanctorum, Maii* tom. vii. p. 103.}

It is quite obvious, however, that if these Books contained the Doctrine for which they are quoted by *Wycliffe,* (viz. that the Year 1400 was to be the Date of the Revelation of *Antichrist,*) they could not have been genuine Productions of the Abbot *Joachim.* The Opinion of *Joachim* was, that the Year 1256 would be the Era of the total Extinction of the Christian Church, and that the Triumph of *Antichrist* was then to commence, and to continue for three Years and a half, counting from the Middle of the Year 1256, to the End of the year 1260. As in the Lines : —

MS. *Har-leian.* Num. 1280. 8. fol. 227.

Hoc Cistercienni Joachim *prædixit in anno*
Quo Saladinus *sanctum sibi subdidit Urbem,*
Cum fuerint anni completi mille ducenti,
Et seni decies a partu Virginis *almæ,*
Tunc Antichristus *nascetur demone plenus.*

Rev. xi. 3, xii. 6.

This Theory was derived from the famous 1260 Days of Prophecy, taking Days for Years, and computing from the Commencement of the common Christian Era. But when the Year 1260 passed away and the Prophecy was not fulfilled, the Followers of *Joachim* attempted to correct the Hypothesis of their Master, and many of them (as for Example the *Beguins,* who adopted the Speculations of *Peter John de Oliva,*) took hold of the 1335 Days of *Daniel,* and from them fixed upon the Year 1335, as the Date of *Antichrist's* Destruction. The Editor has not had Access to any of the Remains of *Peter John's* Writings, but he is informed by a learned

See the *Beguin* Confessions in the *Liber Sententiar. Inquis. Tolos,* pp. 298, 30³, published by *Limborch. Hist. Inquisit.*

Friend, in whose Accuracy he has the fullest Confidence, that *Peter John*, in his *Tracta-* *Tract. de* *tus de Antichristo*, has fixed upon the Year *Antichristo,* *fol. 48, b.* 1356, as the Year of the Revelation, not the Destruction, of *Antichrist*, by adding 96, the supposed Date of the *Apocalypse*, to 1260. *Joachim*, however, in greater Conformity with Scripture, made the Termination of the 1260 Days, (or Years, as he considered them,) the Period of the End, not of the Beginning of *Antichrist*. Our Author's Theory, supported See p. xxvii, by a Cabbalistic Computation from the Let- *et seq.* ters of the Alphabet, which the Editor has not been able to discover elsewhere, makes the Year 1400 the Era of the Revelation of *Anti- christ;* and *Walter Brute*, in 1390, appears *Fox's* Acts to have put forward a Conclusion not very and Monu- ments, vol. dissimilar, although maintained on different i. p. 545. Grounds. His Argument was drawn from the *Lond. fol.* 1684. *Joachitic* Theory of the prophetic Days taken for Years, and from the Supposition that the 1335 Days of *Daniel* commenced at the Desolation of the Temple under *Adrian*.

On the whole then it is unquestionable, that *Wycliffe* had before him some spurious Productions of *Beguinism*, circulated under the Name of the Abbot *Joachim*, but which could not possibly have been derived from the genuine Writings of that Enthusiast. None of these spurious Books, so far as the Editor's limited Means of Research have enabled him to ascertain, have been preserved in our Libraries, or are noticed by the Authors who treat of the Doctrines of *Joachim* and his Successors.

It is evident from p. xxxi, that the Tract before us was composed in or after the Year 1356, the fatal Year of the Revelation of *Antichrist*, according to the Followers of *Peter John*.

Ibid. line 9.

𝕿𝖍𝖊 𝖘𝖊𝖚𝖞𝖓𝖙𝖞 𝖆𝖓𝖉 𝖓𝖞𝖓𝖊 𝖈𝖍𝖆𝖕𝖎𝖙𝖗𝖊.

The Passage quoted is taken from the nine-
tieth *Psalm,* as it is numbered in the *Latin*
Vulgate, (ninety-first in our *English* Version.)
The Editor is not aware of any Reason why
this *Psalm* should be referred to as " the se-
venty and ninth Chapter," and he is, therefore,
constrained to assume, that there is here a Mistake of the Transcriber, who, perhaps, had
before him numeral Letters or Figures, which
he read erroneously. The Words referred to
are to be found in Verses 5 and 6. *Non ti-
mebis a timore nocturno. A sagitta volante
in die, a negotio perambulante in tenebris:
ab incursu, et dæmonio meridiano.*

Ibid. line 11.

𝕬𝖓𝖉 𝕭𝖊𝖗𝖓𝖆𝖗𝖉 𝖆𝖈𝖈𝖔𝖗𝖉𝖎𝖕 𝖕𝖊𝖗𝖊 𝖜𝖎𝖕.

Opp. S. Bernardi. Ed. Bened. p. 1396. C. tom. iv.

The Passage here referred to will be found in St. *Bernard's* Works, Serm. xxxiii. *in Cantica,* num. 14, et seq. *Adhuc nisi tædio fuerit longitudo sermonis, has quatuor tentationes tentabo suo ordine assignare ipsi corpori Christi, quod est Ecclesia. Et ecce quam brevius possum percurro. Videte primitivam Ecclesiam, si non primo pervasa est acriter nimis* a timore nocturno. *Erat enim nox, quando omnis qui interficeret sanctos, arbitrabatur obsequium se præstare Deo. Hac autem tentatione devicta, et sedata tempestate, inclyta facta est, et juxta promissionem ad se factam, in brevi posita in superbiam sæculorum. Et dolens inimicus quod frustra-*

tus esset, a timore nocturno *convertit se cal-lide ad sagittam* volantem in die, *et vulneravit in ea quosdam de ecclesia. Et surrexerunt homines vani, cupidi gloriæ, et voluerunt sibi facere nomen: et exeuntes de ecclesia, diu eamdem matrem suam afflixerunt in diversis et perversis dogmatibus. Sed hæc quoque pestis depulsa est in sapientia sanctorum, si-cut et prima in patientia martyrum.*

PAGE 25, line 7.

chaffare walkynge in derknessis is the prynui heresie of symonyans.

Here our Author abandons St. *Bernard's* In-terpretation, which expounds *negotium peram-bulans in tenebris,* not of Simony, but of Hypo-crisy, and Avarice. *Serpit hodie putida tabes* In Cant.
per omne corpus Ecclesiæ, et quo latius, eo Serm. xxxiii. s. 15.

F

*desperatius: eoque periculosius, quo interius
. . . . . omnes quæ sua sunt quærunt. Mi-
nistri Christi sunt, et serviunt Antichristo.
Honorati incedunt de bonis Domini, qui Do-
mino honorem non deferunt. Inde is quem
quotidie vides meretricius nitor, histrionicus
habitus, regius apparatus. . . . . Inde
dolia pigmentaria, inde referta marsupia.
Pro hujusmodi volunt esse et sunt ecclesia-
rum præpositi, decani, archidiaconi, episcopi,
archiepiscopi. Nec enim hæc merito cedunt,
sed negotio illi, quod perambulat in tenebris.*

Ibid. last line.

on Iȝue.

Cant. Tales.   As *Chaucer.*
v. 3041.
        And here-againes no Creature on live
        Of no degree availleth for to strive.

On live is now contracted or corrupted into

alive. Thus we say, *a-coming, a-saying, a-board, a-purpose, a-sleep, a-way,* &c., for *on* coming, *on* saying, *on* board, *on* purpose, &c. By which it appears that Dr. *Wallis* is mistaken in supposing this Class of Words to be compounded with the Preposition *at.* *Wallisii* Gram. Anglic. p. 86. *Lond.* 8vo. 1765.

John Hopkins, in his Version of Psalm lxxvii. 16, has retained the old Form, *on trembling,* for *a-trembling ;*

> " The Waters, Lord, perceived thee,
> The Waters saw thee well,
> And they for Feare away did flee
> The Depths on trembling fell."

Numerous instances will be found in *Chau-cer,* as, Cant. Tales. v. 1689.

> " On hunting ben they ridden really."

and again, *Ibid.* v. 13666, 7.

> " He could hunt as the wilde dere,
> And ride on hauking for the rivere."

F 2

PAGE xxvi. line 2.

ħabeþ.

This Word should probably be *haven ;* but it is *haveth* in the MS. In the next Line, " byngȳnge," for " bygynnynge," is an obvious Mistake of the MS.

Ibid. line 9.

weren two and twenty hundriddis of ȝeerſs.

By this Date the Writer probably intended the Interval from the Birth of *Heber,* to the Birth of CHRIST : which by the Computation of *Bede* in his *Chronicon sive de sex ætatibus mundi,* wanted but five Years of 2200, a mere Trifle with such Expounders of Prophecy as our Author.

Ibid. line 12.

𝕰𝖚𝖘𝖊𝖇𝖎, 𝕭𝖊𝖉𝖊, & 𝕳𝖆𝖞𝖒𝖔𝖚𝖓𝖉.

The Works here referred to are, probably, the *Chronicon* of *Eusebius*, translated
and preserved by St. *Jerome ;* the venerable
*Bede's Chronicon, sive de sex ætatibus mun-
di ;* and the *Historiæ Ecclesiasticæ Brevia-
rium, sive de Christianarum rerum memo-
ria, Libb. X.* of *Haymo,* Bishop of *Halber-
stadt,* who died A.D. 853.

Opp. B. *Hieronymi.* tom. viii. Ed. *Vallar-sii.*

Page xxvii. line 5.

fro þe begynnynge of 𝕷atin lettris.

That is to say, from the Foundation of
Rome. The Writer speaks in round Num-
bers.

Ibid. line 15.

demynge.

This Word is perhaps a Mistake of the Transcriber for *demed*, i. e. *deemed, considered.*

PAGE xxviii. line 8.

and pes ben berse of .m. lettre.

The Editor has not been able to find these Verses elsewhere. The Letters of the Alphabet are represented as *Collegæ*, or Members of a College, all the rest of whom go forth when the Gates are open; one only, viz. *m*, when they are shut. *College* is for *Collegæ*.

PAGE xxix. line 3.

but bí helpe of Poul.

This alludes to the well-known Story, told
by a great Number of the Antients, of the
Destruction of *Simon Magus,* by the Prayers
of Saints *Peter* and *Paul. Sulpitius Seve-* Sacræ Hist.
rus relates this Event in the following Words: lib. ii. p. 95, 12mo.
Etenim tum illustris illa adversus Simo- Amstel.
nem, Petri ac Pauli congressio fuit. Qui 1695.
cum magicis artibus, ut se Deum probaret,
duobus suffultus dæmoniis evolasset, oratio-
nibus Apostolorum fugatis dæmonibus, de-
lapsus in terram, populo inspectante dis-
ruptus est. The same Account is given by
St. *Cyrill* of *Jerusalem;* after stating that Catech. vi.
Simon had so far succeeded in deceiving the 14.
Romans, that the Emperor *Claudius* had
erected a Statue to him with the Inscription

ΣΙΜΩΝΙ ΘΕΩ ʽΑΓΙΩ, he adds: " The Error spreading, that goodly Pair, Peter and Paul, the Rulers of the Church, being present, set Matters right again; and on Simon, the supposed God, attempting a Display, they straightway laid him dead. Simon, that is, promised that he should be raised aloft towards Heaven, and accordingly was borne through the Air on a Chariot of Dæmons; on which, the Servants of God falling on their Knees, gave an Instance of that Agreement, of which JESUS said, *If two of you shall agree as touching any Thing that they shall ask, it shall be done for them :* and reaching the Sorcerer with this Unanimity of their Prayer, they precipitated him to the Earth."

For other Authorities, see the Note of the *Benedictine* Editor of St. *Cyrill,* on this Passage, and *Tillemont, Memoires pour servir a*

Library of the Fathers, (vol. ii. Transl.) 8vo. *Oxford,* 1838. p. 68.

Matt. xviii. 19.

Opp. B. Cyril. fol. Par. 1720, p. 96.

l'Histoire Ecclesiastique ; Saint Pierre, Tom. i. Art. 34. p. 176.

Ibid. line 6.

𝕮rist sdjal clanse his 𝕮hirche.

In the Original this is, " Chirche schal clanse his Chirche;" the Editor has not hesitated to correct so obvious a Mistake.

PAGE xxx. line 1.

the debel of myddan.

Demonium meridianum, alluding to Ps. xc. 6, in the Vulgate.

Ibid. line 6.

whefore.

A Mistake of the MS. for *Wherefore.*

Ibid. line 10.

in derkenessis.

The Word *in* was omitted by the Original Scribe; but is added in the MS. by a more recent Hand.

Ibid. line 12.

Bede upon the profetis of Sibille.

This Reference is to some spurious Work attributed to *Bede*, and which is probably not the same as the Tract *De Sybillis*, published among *Bede's* Works, and also by *Joh. Opsopæus Brettanus*, at the End of his Edition of the Sybilline Oracles; for that Tract does not contain any thing like the Computation from the Latin Letters, for which *Bede* is here referred to by our Author.

Sibyllina Oracula ex vett. Codd. Aucta, &c. a Joh. Ops. Brettanno, 8vo. Paris, 1607, p. 515.

PAGE xxxi. line 8.

Goddis chirche is foundid in kynrade of prelatis.

This Expression is illustrated by the Preamble of the *Statute of Provisors*, (25 *Edw.* III.): " Whereas late in the Parliament of good Memory of *Edward* King of *England*, Grandfather to our Lord the King that now is, the xxv. [*leg.* xxxv.] Year of his Reign, holden at *Carlisle*, the Petition heard, put before the said Grandfather and his Council, in his said Parliament, by the Communalty of the said Realm, containing : That whereas the Holy Church of *England* was founden in the Estate of Prelacy, within the Realm of *England*, &c."

Statutes of the Realm, vol. i. p. 316.

Gibson's Codex, p. 65.

Ibid. line 13.

𝔂𝔢 𝔴𝔥𝔦𝔠𝔥𝔢 𝔪𝔞𝔶 𝔴𝔢𝔩 𝔟𝔢 𝔠𝔩𝔢𝔭𝔦𝔡 𝔠𝔬𝔩𝔩𝔦𝔟𝔦𝔰𝔱𝔢.

Collybiste, from the Greek Word κολλύβιστης, which is used St. *Matt.* xxi. 12, where St. *Je-*

B. *Hieron.* in Matt. xxi. 12, 13, tom. vii. Ed. *Val- larsii,* 4to. *Venet.* 1769, Col. 162.

rome remarks: *Sed quia erat lege præceptum, ut nemo usuras acciperet, et prodesse non pote- rat pecunia fœnerata, quæ commodi nihil ha- beret, et interdum sortem perderet, excogita- verunt et aliam technam, ut pro nummulariis,* Collybistas *facerent, cujus verbi proprietatem Latina lingua non exprimit.* Collyba *dicun- tur apud eos, quæ nos appellamus* tragemata, *vel vilia munuscula. Verbi gratia, frixi ciceris, uvarumque passarum, et poma di- versi generis.*

See also *Du Cange,* Glossarium, vv. *Colli- bium, Collybista.*

Page xxxii. line 1.

schal be seyd in a manere of careyne.

Careyne, from the old French, *carogne, carrion;* " seyd in a manere of careyne," perhaps may mean, " they shall be spoken of as a Sort of Carrion," unless there be here some Mistake of the Transcriber, which is not improbable. The next Clause, " thei schal be cast out as dogge in myddis places," is possibly an Allusion to *Is.* v. 25. *Et facta sunt morticinia eorum, quasi stercus in medio platearum;* the Word *dogge* being a Mistake for *donge;* and, "in myddis places" the Author's Version of *in medio platearum;* although it is highly probable that *myddis* is corrupt.

Ibid. line 3.

𝔥𝔢𝔯 𝔴𝔦𝔭 𝔞𝔠𝔬𝔯𝔡𝔦𝔭 ℭ𝔞𝔯𝔫𝔬𝔰𝔢𝔫𝔰𝔦𝔰.

John of Salisbury, called *Carnotensis,* be-
cause he was Bishop of *Chartres.* The Passage referred to occurs in his *Polycraticus,*
sive De Nugis Curialium, Lib. vii. *cap.* 20.
Si dicas quia ignis per septuaginta annos
Babylonicæ captivitatis sub aqua vixerat,
demum extinctus est, Antiocho *vendente Ja-*
soni sacerdotium; aut quod Beatus Gregorius
testatur, quia pestilentia et fames, concussio-
nes gentium, collisiones regnorum, et quam-
plurima adversa terris proveniunt, ex eo quod
honores ecclesiastici ad pretium vel humanam
gratiam conferuntur personis non meritis.
The other Reference (Line 11) is to *Lib.* viii.
cap. 18. *Nam et peccata populi faciunt reg-*

Polycrat. p.
491. *Lugd.*
Bat. 1639,
8vo.

Ibid. p.
635.

nare hypocritam, et sicut Regum testatur his-
toria, defectus sacerdotum, in populo Dei, ty-
rannos induxit.

Ibid. line 10.

bep geue.

A Mistake probably for *ben geve,* i. e. *been*
given.

Ibid. line 16.

alle children boren sippen pe first
pestilence, &c.

The Year 1348 and two following Years
are recorded in all our Chronicles, as remarka-
ble for a most formidable Pestilence which
devastated Europe, and is said to have been
attended with this singular Circumstance,
that the Children born after the Pestilence

See *Bocca-*
cio Deca-
meron,
Giorn, 1[ma]

had begun, were found to be deficient in the usual Number of Teeth. It may be enough to quote from our English Annalists, the Chronicle of *Caxton.* Speaking of the 23rd Year of King *Edward* the Third, the Historian says: " ¶ And in the xxiij Yere of his Regne, in yᵉ East Partyes of the Worlde, there began a Pestylence and Deth of Sarasyns and Paynyms, that so grete a Deth was never herde of afore, and that wasted away the People, so that unneth the tenth Persone was left alive. ¶ And in the same Yere, about yᵉ South Countrees there fell so moche Rayne, and so grete Waters, that from Chrystmasse unto Mydsomer there was unnethes no Daye nor Nyght but that rayned somewhat, through which Waters yᵉ Pestilence was so enfected, and so haboundant in all Countrees, and namely, about yᵉ Court of Rome, and other Places, and See Costes, that unneth

Caxton's Chronicle, fol. Lond. 1528, fol. c.xxiii.a.

there were lefte lyuyng Folke for to bury them honestly y^t were deed. But made grete Diches and Pyttes y^t were wonders brode and depe, and therin buryed them, and made a Renge of deed Bodyes, and cast a lytell Erth to couer them aboue, and than cast in another Renge of deed Bodyes, and another Renge aboue them. And thus were they buryed, and none other wyse, but yf it were so y^t they were Men of grete Estate, so that they were buryed as honestly as they myght."   And again, " And in this same Yere," [24 *Edw.* III.] " and in the Yere afore, and in the Yere nexte folowynge, was so grete a Pestylence of Men from the Eest in to the West, and namely through Botches, y^t they that sekened, as on this Daye, dyed on the thyrde Daye after, to ye whiche Men y^t so dyed in this Pestylence had but lytell Respyte of theyr Lyggynge.   Than Pope *Clement* of his Goodnes and Grace,

Fol. cxxiii. d.

G

gave them full Remyssyon and Forgyuenes
of all theyr Synnes that they were shryuen of,
and this Pestylence lasted in *London* fro Mi-
ghelmasse vnto August nexte followynge, al-
most an hole Yere. And in these Dayes was
Deth without Sorowe, Weddynges without
Frendshyp, wylful Penaunce, and Derth without Scarsete, and Fleynge w^tout Refute or
Sucour, for many fledde from Place to Place
bycause of the Pestylence, but they were in-
fected, and might not escape ye Deth, after y^t
ye Prophete *Isaie* sayth, Who that fleeth fro
the Face of Drede, he shall fall into the
Dyche. And he y^t wyndeth him out of y^e
Dyche, he shall be holden and tyed with a
Grenne. But whan this Pestylence was cesed,
as God wolde, unnethes ye tenth Parte of
the People was left on lyue. ¶ And in
ye same Yere began a wonders thynge, that
all y^t were borne after ye Pestylence had two

Cheketethe in ther Heed lesse than they had afore."

Hollinshed records in like Manner the Fact of the Pestilence, and the Desolation caused by it throughout *Europe.* Of *London* he says that the Death " had bin so great and vehement within that Citie, that over and beside the Bodies buried in other accustomed burieng Places, (which for their infinit Number cannot be reduced into Account), there were buried that Yeare" [viz. 1350] " dailie, from Candlemasse till Easter, in the Charterhouse Yard of *London*, more than two hundred dead Corpses." He also notices the Fact of the Children wanting Teeth, but he makes the Defect to be four, not two " cheke Teeth," as *Caxton's* Chronicle stated: " ¶ This Yeare in August died *Philip de Valois* the French King. Here is to be noted, that all those that were borne after the Beginning of that

Chron. sub. an, 1348, vol. ii. p. 378-9. Lond. 1587.

Ibid. p. 379.

G 2

great Mortalitie whereof ye have heard, wanted foure cheke Teeth (when they came to the time of Growth) of those 32 which the People before that Time commonlie vsed to have, so that they had but 28."

Our Author, it will be observed, differs from *Hollinshed* in making the Defect "eight grete Teeth," and in this he has the Authority of the second Continuator of the Chronicle of *William de Nangis*, published by *D'Achery* in his *Spicilegium ;* a Narrative which apparently has been the Source from which many of our English Chroniclers have borrowed. It contains a very minute History of this memorable Pestilence, with several curious Particulars not mentioned by other Writers. The Author endeavours to account for the Plague by supposing the Explosion of a Comet, whose sudden Evaporation, he suggests, may have disseminated in the Atmosphere pestilential

D'Achery,
Spicileg.
tom. iii. p.
109, sq.

Vapours. He tells us also that the Jews were suspected of having poisoned the Fountains, and that many of them were in consequence put to Death, and burnt, in various Places. The circumstance of the Children born with a smaller Number of Teeth is thus recorded:—

Cessante autem dictâ epidemiâ, pestilentiâ, Ibid. p. 110. *et mortalitate, nupserunt viri qui remanserunt et mulieres ad invicem, conceperunt uxores residuæ per mundum ultrà modum, nulla sterilis efficiebatur, sed prægnantes hinc inde videbantur, et plures geminos pariebant, et aliquæ tres infantes insimul vivos emittebant; sed quod ultra modum admirationem facit, est quod dicti pueri nati post tempus illud mortalitatis supradictæ, et deinceps, dum ad ætatem dentium devenerunt, non nisi viginti dentes vel viginti duos in ore communiter habuerunt, cum ante dicta tempora homines de communi cursu triginta duos dentes,*

*sub et supra, simul in mandibulis habuissent.
Quid autem numerus iste dentium in post
natis significet, multum miror, nisi dicatur,
quod per talem et tantam mortalitatem hominum infinitorum et successionem aliorum et
reliquorum qui remanserant, mundus est quo-
dammodo renovatus et seculum, ut sic sit
quædam nova ætas ; sed proh dolor ! ex
hujus renovatione seculi non est mundus prop-
ter hoc in melius commutatus. Nam homines
fuerunt postea magis avari et tenaces, cum
multo plura bona quam antea possiderent ;
magis etiam cupidi, et per lites brigas et rixas
atque per placita seipsos conturbantes, nec
per hujusmodi terribilem mortis pestem a Deo
inflictam fuit pax inter Reges et dominos re-
formata, quinimo inimici Regis Franciæ ac
etiam guerræ Ecclesiæ fortiores et pejores
quam ante per mare et per terram suscitave-
runt, et mala ampliora ubique pullularunt.*

Et quod iterum mirabile fuit; nam cum omnis abundantia omnium bonorum esset, cuncta tamen cariora in duplo fuerunt, tam de rebus utensilibus, quam de victualibus, ac etiam de mercimoniis et mercenariis et agricolis et servis, exceptis aliquibus hereditatibus et domibus quæ superflue remanserant his diebus. Charitas etiam ab illo tempore refrigescere cœpit valde, et iniquitas abundavit cum ignorantiis et peccatis: nam pauci inveniebantur qui scirent aut vellent in domibus, villis, et castris, informare pueros in grammaticalibus rudimentis.

The Allusion contained in the Tract before us to the Circumstance of the Children wanting Teeth, may possibly be urged as an Objection to the early Date of 1350, which it claims for itself. For if this Circumstance of the Want of Teeth be a Fable, it is not probable that it could so soon have become current;

and if on the other hand it be true, it seems hardly possible that the Fact could have been ascertained in 1350, respecting all Children born *since* the first Pestilence, i. e. since 1348. However, it is possible that by the *first* Pestilence our Author may have alluded, not to that of 1348, but to that of 1340, which is thus described by Knighton, under that Year: "*In æstate scilicet anno gratiæ* M.CCC.XL., *accidit quædam execrabilis et enormis infirmitas in* Anglia *quasi communis, et præcipue in comitatu* Leicestriæ, *adeo quod durante passione homines emiserunt vocem latrabilem ac si esset latratus canum; et fuit quasi intolerabilis pœna durante passione. Exinde fuit magna pestilentia hominum.*"

It is no Doubt a Difficulty that the Continuator of *William de Nangis* and other Chroniclers, represent the Phenomenon of the Want of Teeth as the Consequence of the Pestilence

De event.
Angliæ.
(Apud x.
Script.)
Col. 2580.

of 1348, but the Story may have originated at the former Period, although later Writers recorded it in Connexion with the more recent and more formidable Pestilence.

The Editor, however, leaves this Question to be decided by future Research, and by Judges more competent than himself. It is not impossible that the whole Passage in which See p. xxxi. the Date of " thrittene hundrid yere and sixe and fifty" has been given, may prove to be a Quotation from the Book referred to under the Title of " *Joachim* in the Book of the Seedis of Profetis," and if so, the Tract before us must of course be the Production of a later Period.

PAGE xxxiii. line 1.

Merlin Ambrose.

For the History of *Merlyn,* see *Geoffrey* of

Monmouth's Historia Regum Britanniæ, Lib.
vi. c. 17, 18. The famous Prophecy of *Merlyn*
will be found in Lib. vii. c. 3, 4. It has also
been repeatedly published in a separate Form,
with the Commentaries in seven Books of
Alanus de Insulis.

Ibid. line 3.

of þe myscheif.

In the original MS. these Words are re-
peated, " *in - the tyme of the myscheif of the
myscheif of the Kok ;*" the Editor did not
deem it necessary to retain so obvious a Mistake of the Transcriber.

Ibid. line 5.

þe sixte of irlond.

This Personage is mentioned in numerous

Prophecies circulated under the Names of *Merlyn, Gildas, Robert of Bridlington, Sybill,* and others, in the fourteenth and fifteenth Centuries, many of which appear to have had their Origin in the Prophecy of *Merlyn,* pre-served by *Geoffrey* of *Monmouth,* already re-ferred to, where we find " the sixte of *Irlond*" thus noticed :—

Sextus Hiberniæ *mœnia subvertet, et nemora in planitiem mutabit : Diversas portiones in unum reducet, et capite leonis coronabitur.* *Galf. Mon-muthen.* lib. vii. c. 3, ap. *Rer. Brit-tan. Scrip-tores.* p. 50. *Heidelb.* 1587.

The following Collection of Prophecies re-lating to *Sextus* of *Ireland,* is from a MS. written about the Middle of the Fourteenth Century, and preserved in the Library of *Trinity College, Dublin.*

Iste sunt prophetie diuerse a diuersis pro-phetate de Sexto Hibernie, *quivocatur Dominus* [here there is an erasure in the MS.] *Rex* An-glie *et* Francie *et* Sextus *Dominus* Hibernie, *de* *Cod.* MS. *in Bibl.* Coll. SS. Trin. Dubl. *Cl.* B. *Tab.* 2, *No.* 7, fol. 209.

quo Prophetie sunt notate. Hermerus *Dominus*
sapientum. Anno a Creatione mundi sex

Vid. *Contin.* M.CCC *et* IIII ^{XX} Lilium *regnans in nobiliore*
altera Chro- *mundi mouebit se contra senem leonem, et veniet*
nici Gul. de
Nangis, *ap.* *in terram eius inter spinas regni sui, et cir-*
Dacherii *cumdabit filium leonis illo anno ferens feras in*
Spicil. t.iii.
104, *where* *brachio suo.* Cuius *regnum erit in terra lune*
this *Prophe-* *timendus per vniuersum mundum potestate*
cy *is attri-*
buted *to* *agentis principalis, cum magno exercitu suo*
Johannes de
Muis. *transiet aquas et gradietur in terram leonis*
carentis auxilio, quia bestie regionis sue iam
dentibus suis eius pellem dilaceraverint. Illo
anno veniet Aquila a parte orientali, alis ex-
tensis super solem, cum multitudine pullorum
suorum, in adiutorium Filii hominis. Illo anno
Aquila destruetur. Amor magnus erit in
mundo. Una die in quadam parte leonis erit
bellum inter plures reges crudeles, quod usque
ad diem illum non viderunt homines ; illa die
erit sanguinis diluvium, et perdet Lilium coro-

nam solis, quam accepit Aquila, de qua Filius hominis postmodum coronabitur. Per quatuor annos sequentes fient multa in mundo prelia inter omnes homines fidem tenentes, quia illo tempore credenda sunt. Omnia tunc erint communia. Maior pars mundi destruetur, caput mundi erit ad terram declinatum. Filius hominis et Aquila relevabunt ille [sic], *et tunc erit pax in toto orbe terrarum, et copia fructuum, et filius hominis mare transiet, et portabit signum mirabile ad terram promissionis, sed prima causa sibi permissa remanebit.*

Item versus illius sompniatoris viri religiosi, per quos versus cognoscitur Sextus Hiberniæ.

Illius imperium gens barbara senciet illum,
Roma *volet tanto principe digna dici,*
Conferet hic Rome *plus laudis quam sibi* Roma,
Plus dabit hic orbi quam dabit orbis ei.

Versus vaticinales de Normannia, *de eodem* Sexto.
Anglia *transmittet Leopardum lilia Galli,*

Qui pede calcabit Cancrum cum fratre su-
  perbo,
Ungues diripient Leopardi Gallica regna,
Circulus inuictus circumdabit unde peribunt.
Anglia *regnabit*, Vasconia *porta redibit*
Ad iuga consueta Leopardi Flandria *magna*
*Flumina concipient que confundent gene-
  tricem.*
Lilia marcescent, Leopardi posse vigebit,
Ecclesie sub quo libertas prima redibit.
Huic Babilon *veniet truces aras non teret
  omnes,*
Acon Ierusalem *Leopardi posse redempte,*
Ad cultum fidei gaudebunt se redituras,
Imperium mundi sub quo dabit hic heremita.

Versus cuiusdem nomine Gildas, *per quantum tempus regnabit idem* Sextus.

Ter tria lustra tenent cum semi tempora
  Sexti,
En vagus in primo perdet, sub fine resumet,

Multa rapit medio volitans sub fine secundi,
Orbem submittet reliquo, clerumque reducet
Ad statum primum, post hoc renouat loca
  sancta
Hinc terram spernens secundo ethere scandit.

In another MS. in the Library of *Trinity* Cod. MS. *in*
College, Dublin, there is preserved a Pro- *Bibl.* Coll.
SS. Trin.
phecy in which *Sextus* of *Ireland* is also Dubl. *Class.*
mentioned, and which, as the Editor is in- E. *Tab.* 5,
No. 10, fol.
formed by his learned Friend *John Holmes,* xliii.
Esq., of the *British Museum,* occurs also in
the *Arundel* MS. 57, fol. 4, b., where it is
entitled, *"Versus Gylde de Prophetia Aquile."*
It will suffice to quote from this Prophecy
the Lines where *Sextus* is mentioned.
Sextus Hybernensis *milleno milite cinctus,*
  Hostibus expulsis castra relicta petet,
Menia subversa vix antrix apta ferarum
  Pinget et eiectus bubo necabit apem.

Ibid.

𝔭𝔢 𝔴𝔦𝔱𝔱 𝔦𝔰 𝔬𝔲𝔯 𝔨𝔦𝔫𝔤 𝔴𝔦𝔭 𝔥𝔦𝔰 𝔠𝔥𝔦𝔩𝔡𝔯𝔢𝔫.

" *The witt*," i. e. the Meaning; alluding probably to the Interpretation given of this part of the Prophecy by *Alanus de Insulis*, who supposes the then reigning King Henry II. and his Sons to be intended ; his Words are ·—

Prophetia Anglicana vii. Libris explana-tionum *Alani de Insulis.* Francof. 1603. 12ᵐᵒ. lib. iii. p. 91.

Henricus *qui nunc in* Anglia *regnat, quinque filios suscepit ex Regina conjuge sua, quorum unus mortuus est, quatuor vero supersunt. Habuit et sextum ex concubina, qui clericus est, magnæ, ut aiunt, juxta ælatem, probitatis. Hic itaque vel sextus dicetur Henrici Regis filius, si mortuus ille quem habuit ex Regina inter alios computetur, vel quintus, si soli superstites a propheta numerantur, et alius adhuc expectandus, quem hic* Sextum *appellat. Possumus tamen sextum istum intelligere, qui in* Anglia *regnaturus sit post quatuor istos, et alium quintum quicunque ille sit, hoc est sive istorum frater, sive non, de quo dicitur quod* Hyberniæ *sit mænia subversurus, excisurus nemora, et in planitiem mutaturus diversas portiones, id est regna diversa, non est enim unum regnum, sed plura, ad unum regnum reducturus, ejusque coronam, assumpta feritate et fortitudine leonina, suo capite impositurus.*

Ibid. line 9.

𝕾ibille accordip ꜩerto.

The Verses of " Sibille" here quoted arc to be found in a large Collection of other Prophecies of the same character, in a Manuscript of the fourteenth Century, preserved in the Library of *Trinity College, Dublin.* The Editor is also enabled, through the Kindness of Mr. *Holmes,* to give here a complete Copy of them from the *Cotton*

Cod. MS. in Biblioth Coll. SS. Trin. Dublin. Class. L. Tab. 5, No. 10.

H

MS. *Claud.* B. vii., collated with the *Arundel* MS. 57, fol. In this latter MS. which is written, as Mr. *Holmes* conjectures, in a Hand of about the Year 1350, and also in the *Dublin* MS. the Line *Terræ motus, &c.* comes immediately before the Line *Millenis ducentenis.* The other various Readings are given in the Margin; A. denoting the *Arundel*, and D. the *Dublin* Manuscript.

[a] *Deest titul. in Cod. Dublin.*

      " Sybilla *de eventibus regnorum et eorum Regum ante finem mundi.*" [a]

Gallorum *lenitas* Germanos *iustificabit,*
Italiæ *gravitas* Gallos *confusa necabit.*

[b] *Gallus* succumbet. A. D.

Succumbet Gallus [b], Aquilæ *victricia* [c] *signa*

[c] Victoria. D.
[d] Abhorrebit. D.

Mundus *adorabit,* [d] *erit urbs sub* [e] *presule digna.*

[e] Vox. D.
[f] Aliis. D.

Millenis ducentenis nonaginta sub annis,
Et tribus [f] *adiunctis, consurget aquila grandis.*

Terræ motus erunt, quos[g] *non procul*[h] *augu-*
ror esse.

Constantine *cades, et equi de marmore facti,*
Et lapis erectus, et multa palatia Rome.
Papa cito moritur, Cesar *regnabit ubique,*
Sub quo tunc vana cessabit gloria[i] *cleri.*
Anno millesimo C.ter vicesimo v. dabit ether
Blada vina fractus fiet pro principe luctus ;
Una columpna cadet, quæ terram schismate
tradet,
Gens periet subito, Petro *testante perito.*

The last four Verses occur only in the *Dub-lin* MS., and seem to contain an Allusion to the Prophetical Doctrines of *Peter John,* or rather of his Followers. The Date intended is probably 1325, taking " *C.ter*" for CCC ; and that this Year was one of the Eras fixed by the *Beguins* for the Revelation of Antichrist, appears from the *Liber Sententiarum Inqui-sitionis Tholosanæ,* published by Limborch ;

[g] Erit, quem. A.
[h] Plus. A.

[i] Cessabunt gaudia. D.

Limborch. *Hist. In-quisit. ad fin.* p. 303.

for Example *Petrus Moresii,* a Beguin, *recep-
tus ad tercium ordinem Sancti Francisci conju-
gatus,* was examined by the Inquisitors on the
8th of April, 1322, and declares, *Credidit et
credebat firmiter, tempore quo captus fuit,
quod Antichristus esset venturus, et consump-
maturus cursum suum, infra annum quo com-
putabitur incarnacio Domini* M.CCC.XXV.

The Verses, as quoted by our Author, are
very corrupt in the Original MS. The Editor
has therefore ventured to alter *"viccus"* into
" victricia ;" " urbis" into *" urbs,"* and
" tessabit" into *" cessabit."*

Ibid. last line.

clispiriu.

This Word is very probably corrupt, although
Lewis, who appears to have received from *Dublin* a Transcript of this Tract, or copious Ex-

tracts, does not seem to have considered it so,
for he has inserted the Word in his *Glossary*,
and quotes for it only the Authority of the
Passage before us ; he says,

" *Elispired*, perhaps for *expired. Secular* Hist. of the
power of the Hooly Goost expired, alluding to Life of *Wiclif.* Oxf.
the secular Power the Popes have. For having 1820.
quoted four Verses of *Sibille*, one of which is : *(Table of obsolete*
Papa cito moritur, Cæsar regnabit ubique, *Words;* in voc.)
Wiclif adds, *thei that treten this Verse of*
Sibille, *alle that I have seen, accorden in this,*
that secular power of the Hooly Goost elis-
pired."

PAGE xxxiv. line 13.

þe wordís of Josue 2. cᵒ. þe pridde.

The Editor is unable to explain this Reference.

Ibid. line 17.

ꝑe 𝔐ayster of 𝔖cholys rehersiy.

Peter Comestor, Chancellor of the Cathedral of *Paris* in 1164, and Author of the *Historia Scholastica,* is the Person here called *Master of Schools.* The Passage referred to occurs in the *Hist. Schol.* on the third Book of Kings, *cap. viii.* (not *cap. v.* as quoted by our Author), and is as follows :—

Petri Co-
mestoris
Hist. Schol.
8o. Florent.
1526. fol.
cxvii.

Fabulantur Iudei *ad eruderandos lapides celerius habuisse* Salomonem *sanguinem ver- miculi qui* Tamir *dicitur : quo aspersa mar- mora facile secabantur, quem invenit hoc modo.* ¶ *Erat* Salomoni *strutio habens pul- lum, et inclusus est pullus sub vase vitreo. Quem cum videret strutio, sed habere nequiret: de deserto tulit vermiculum: cuius sanguine liniuit vitrum, et fractum est.*

The same Story with the very same mystical Application of it which is made by our Author, is given by *Peter Berchorius* in his *Reductorium morale*, who quotes from *Gervase* of *Tilbury*. This latter Writer, as we learn from *Berchorius*, took the Story from *Peter Comestor*, and being an Englishman, was most probably the immediate Source from which the Author of the Tract before us derived it, especially as *Gervase* wrote upwards of a Century before *Berchorius*, who died in 1362. The Editor has not had an Opportunity of consulting the Work of *Gervase* of *Tilbury*, but it is probable that *Berchorius* has done little more than extract his Words.

De struthione mirabile quid ponit Geruasius, *et videtur accipere de Historia Scholastica. Dicunt* Iudæi (*ut ait) quod cum* Salomon *templum ædificaret, ut lapides citius sculperentur, inclusit pullum struthionis in vase*

Berchorii *Red. Mor.* lib. xiv. c. 60. n. 4. p. 658. fol. Venet. 1683.

*vitreo, quem cum struthio habere nequiret,
ad desertum iuit, et exinde vermem qui* Thamus *dicitur, apportauit, cuius sanguine vitrum liniuit ; fractoque statim vitro, pullum
recuperauit. Quo agnito* Salomon *de sanguine illorum vermium lapides templi fecit
liniri, et sic faciliter potuerunt imprimi vel
sculpi. Idem verò* Geruasius *dicit Romæ in
quodam antiquo palatio fialam liquore lacteo
plenam, esse inuentam, quo liniti lapides
facillimè sculpebantur. Talis vermis videtur
fuisse* Christus. *Pullus enim Struthionis, i.
homo (qui erat per creationem pullus, et
filius Dei Patris) fuerat incarceratus, et
carceri culpæ et pœnæ, a mundi principio
destinatus. Struthio ergo, i. Deus Pater, a
deserto paradisi, vermem, i. Christum hominem factum, adduxit, et ipsum per passionem occidit, vel occidi permisit, et sic cum
isto sanguine portas carceris infernalis fregit,*

et pullum suum hominem liberavit. Zac. 9.
*Tu autem in sanguine testamenti tui eduxisti
vinctos tuos de lacu. Igitur quicunque voluerit lapidem, quicunque cor suum durum et
lapideum, per contritionem scindere, et per
conversationem sculpere decreuerit, adhibeat
sanguinem huius vermis, i. dominicæ passionis
memoriam, et liquorem lacteum memoriæ suæ
benedictæ, et sic nunquam erit ita durum aut
obstinatum, quin recipiat contritionis scissu-
ram, et correctionis sculpturam.* Ezech. 36.
*Auferam cor lapideum de carne vestra, et da-
bo vobis cor carneum.*

The same Story occurs in some Copies of
the *Gesta Romanorum*, where the Artifice by
which the Worm " *thumare,*" (as it is there
called,) was detected, is ascribed to the Emperor *Diocletian* of *Rome.* See *Swan's* Trans-
lation of the *Gesta Romanorum*, vol. I. Introd.
p. lxiv.

*Gesta Ro-
manorum,
&c. transla-
ted from the
Latin by the
Rev. Char-
les Swan.*
2 vols. 12º.
London,
1824.

The Name of the Worm, to which the mar-
vellous Property of breaking Stones is ascribed,
is corruptly given by the foregoing Authorities. It is called by the Jews, not *tamir*, or
thamus, but *schamir* (שמיר), and frequent Allusions to it occur in the Rabbinical Writers.
The original Story is to be found in the *Talmud*, and seems intended to explain what we
read 1 Kings, vi. 7, that *neither Hammer nor
Axe nor any Tool of Iron* was heard in the
Temple of *Solomon* while it was in building.

Talmud   The following is an abridged Account of the
Babyl.
Tract.   original Legend: *Solomon*, when about to
Gittin. fol. build the Temple, perceived by his Wisdom,
68. col. 1, 2. that it would be more acceptable to GOD, if
built of Stones upon which no Tool of Iron
had ever been raised. Whereupon he inquir-
ed of the Rabbis how this was to be effected.—
They told him that he must procure the Worm
Schamir, by the Help of which *Moses* had cut

the Stones of the High Priest's Breastplate. *Solomon* then inquired where this Worm was to be found. The Rabbis confessed their Ignorance, but advised him to summon certain Devils, and compel them, by Torments, to make the Discovery; this was done, and the Devils answered, that *Aschmedai*, the King of the Devils, alone, could tell where the Worm *Schamir* was to be found. Accordingly, *Benaiah*, Son of *Jehoiada*, was sent with a Chain on which the Name of GOD was inscribed, to bind *Aschmedai*, and bring him before *Solomon*. It took some Time to capture *Aschmedai*, and a long Account is given of the Difficulties of the Undertaking. At Length, on the third Day, he is brought to *Solomon*, who asks him for the *Schamir*. *Aschmedai* answers, It is not in my Keeping; but *Sara-Dima* (the Angel that presides over the Sea) has it, and he will entrust it only to the Wild-Hen (תרנגולא),

from whom he exacts an Oath for its safe Return. *Solomon* asked what the Wild-Hen did with the *Schamir*; the Dæmon answered, She brings the Worm to the Rocky Mountains, destitute of Grass and Verdure, and by its means she breaks down their Rocks; she then carries up the Seeds of Trees, and thus the Mountains, once Barren, become covered with Woods. Having obtained this Information *Solomon* sought out the Nest of the Wild-Hen, and enclosed it, with her Young Ones, in a Covering of transparent Crystal. The Wild-Hen, on her Return, seeing her Nest and Young Ones, but finding herself unable to enter it, flew away, and soon after returned with the Worm *Schamir*; whereupon *Solomon's* Servants, who had been lying in Wait for her, set up a great Shout, which so terrified her, that she dropped the Worm, and thus *Solomon* obtained Possession of it. The Wild-Hen, however, flew away, and hanged herself, for having lost the Worm, and broken her Oath. See *Eisenmenger, Entdecktes Judenthum* Theil, I. p. 350. *Johan. Christoph. Wagenseilii Sota,* p. 1072, and *Buxtorfii Lexicon Chald. et Talmud. in voce* שמיר.

Page xxxv. line 1.

after þe talis of iewis of Salamon.

That is, " reherseth, after, or according to, the Tales or Legends of the *Jews*, concerning *Solomon.*"

Ibid. line 8.

the glass to barst.

To, perhaps for "al to," *statim, penitus.* Thus in our *English* Version of the Bible, (Judg. ix. 53.) "And a certain Woman cast a Piece of a Millstone upon *Abimelech's* Head, and al to brake his Skull."

Ibid. line 14.

ye on & twenty Salme. 2í.

The Editor is not sure that he has rightly deciphered the Letters represented by "2í;" he once thought they were "rí," but this seemed inexplicable, and he now believes them to be an Attempt of a very ignorant Transcriber to represent in *Arabic* Numerals the Number of the Psalm referred to.

Page xxxvi. line 15.

Poul writiþ to the Romans.

This Reference belongs to what goes before, not to what follows. Mr. *Vaughan*, in his *Life of Wycliffe*, not perceiving this, has altered *Vol.* i. p. 259. 2nd Edit. the Text to make the Sense perfect, and quotes the Passage thus: "So, when we were sinful, and the Children of Wrath, God's Son came out of Heaven, and praying His Father for His Enemies, He died for us. Then much rather shall we be saved, now we are made righteous through His Blood. St. Paul writeth to the *Romans*, that *Jesus* should pray for us, and that He went into Heaven to appear in the Presence of God for us. The same also he writeth to the *Hebrews*, the which Presence may He grant us to behold, who liveth and reigneth without End.— Amen."

Mr. *Vaughan*, however, does not tell his Readers what Passage of the Epistle to the *Romans*, occurring, also, in the Epistle to the *Hebrews*, he supposes our Author to have quoted. There exists, in Fact, no such Passage ; nor does the Text stand in Need of any Emendation. The References, in both Cases, come after the Passages quoted ; and this removes all the Difficulty which Mr. *Vaughan* appears to have found in the Reading of the original Manuscript.

FINIS.

CPSIA information can be obtained
at www.ICGtesting.com
Printed in the USA
LVOW04s1921250316
480784LV00016B/470/P